VEHICLES

Colour By Number

This book belongs to

Book by Sachin Sachdeva (Author/Illustrator)

1. Black   2. Blue   3. Grey   4. Dark Grey

5. Red   6. Yellow   7. Sky Blue   8. Green

1. Sky Blue   2. White   3. Red   4. Dark Grey
5. Grey   6. Blue   7. Yellow

1. Red   2. Dark Grey   3. Black   4. Sky Blue

5. Green   6. Grey   7. Light Brown   8. Yellow

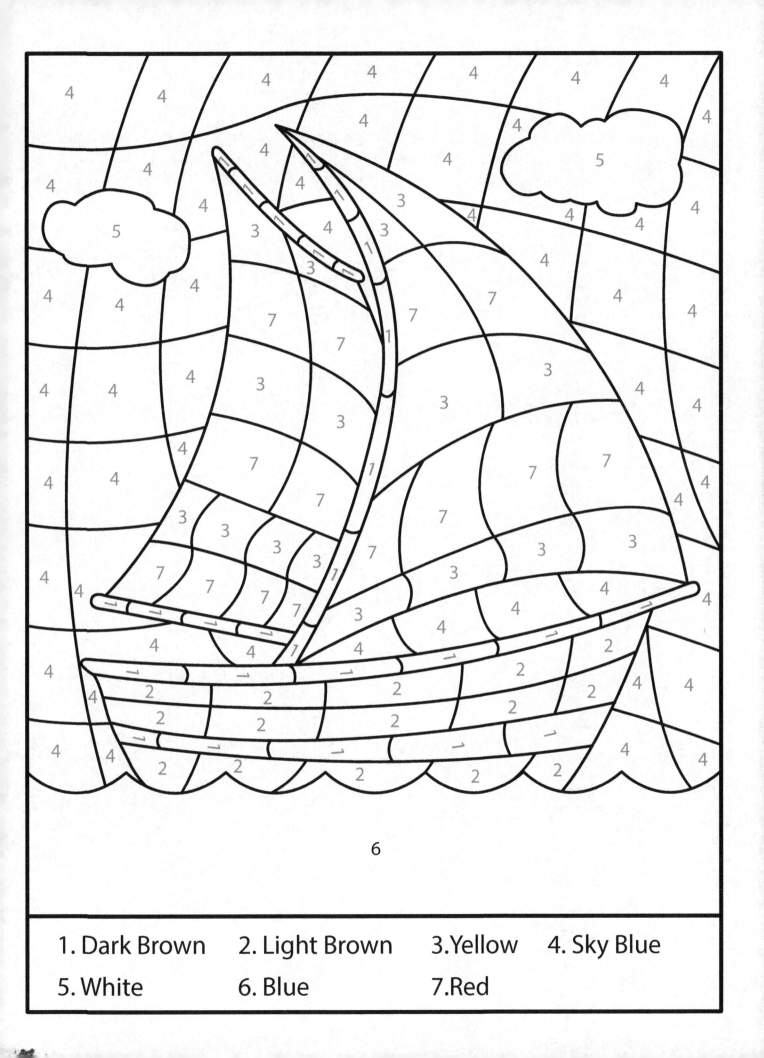

1. Dark Brown   2. Light Brown   3.Yellow   4. Sky Blue
5. White   6. Blue   7.Red

1. Dark Grey   2. Black   3. Yellow   4. Red
5. Light Brown   6. Sky Blue   7. Dark Brown   8. Blue

1. Red   2. Light Grey   3. Grey   4. Dark Grey

5. Orange   6. Yellow   7. Sky Blue

1. Red   2. Green   3. Orange   4. Grey

5. Yellow   6. Light Brown   7. Light Blue

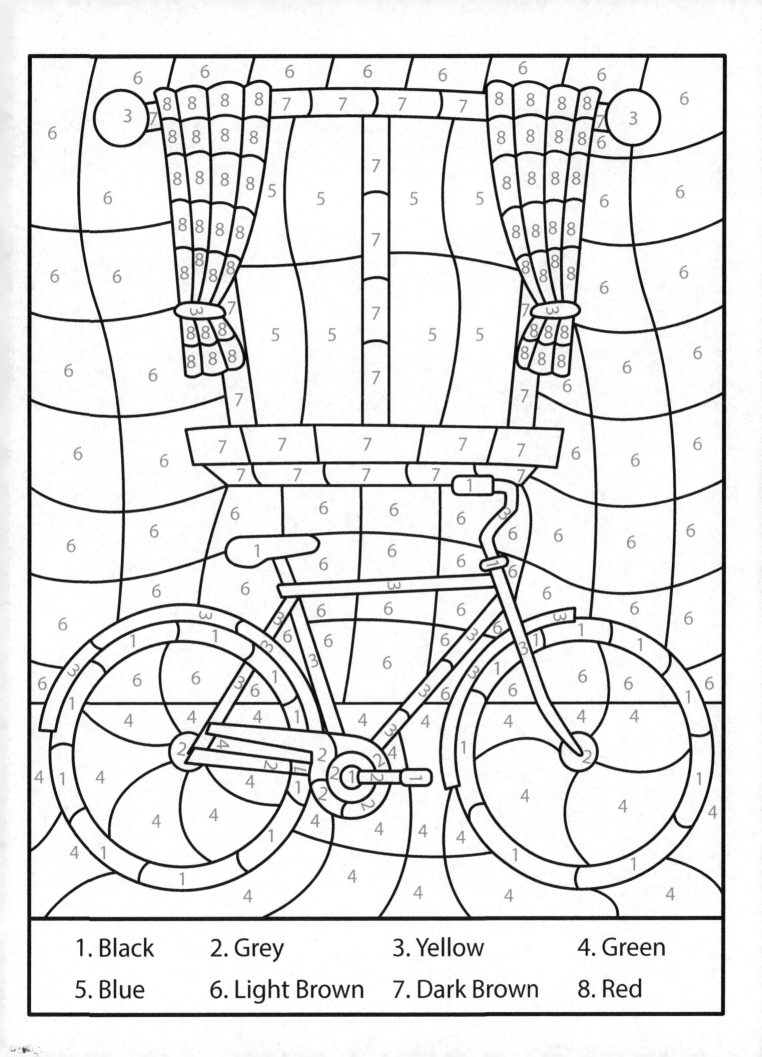

1. Black   2. Grey   3. Yellow   4. Green

5. Blue   6. Light Brown   7. Dark Brown   8. Red

1. Black   2. Blue   3. Yellow   4. Orange

5. Dark Grey   6. Sky Blue   7. Green   8. Light Grey

1. Red 2. Green 3. Sky Blue 4. Light Brown

5. Yellow 6. Dark Brown 7. White

1. Black 2. White 3. Grey 4. Dark Grey
5. Sky Blue 6. Yellow 7. Red 8. Light Brown

1. Black   2. Red   3. Grey   4. Yellow

5. Dark Grey   6. Blue   7. Sky Blue   8. Light Brown

1. Black   2. Yellow   3. Grey   4. Light Green

5. Dark Grey   6. Blue   7. White   8. Green

1. Black   2. Yellow   3. Red   4. Sky Blue
5. Light Brown   6. Blue   7. Dark Brown   8 .Green

1. Black   2. Dark brown   3. Green   4. Grey
5. Dark Grey   6. Blue   7. Light Brown   8. White

1. Black   2. Sky Blue   3. Green   4. Grey

5. Dark Grey   6. Yellow   7. Light Brown   8. Orange

1. Black   2. Red   3. Yellow   4. Light Brown
5. Grey   6. Blue   7. Sky Blue

1.Black   2. White   3. Yellow   4. Light Brown

5. Grey   6. Blue   7. Sky Blue

1. Dark Grey   2. Green   3. Grey   4. Brown

5. Black   6. Red   7. Sky Blue   8. Yellow

1. Black   2. Yellow   3. Green   4. Grey

5. Dark Grey   6. Light Blue   7. Dark Brown   8. Sky Blue

Thank you for purchasing the book. I hope you and your family members enjoyed coloring the pages.

Kindly **leave ratings and feedback** on Amazon so that it will help other people in deciding to purchase my books. I'll be very thankful to you.

If you want to write any personal note, feel free to send email at **sachin@sachinsachdev.com**

I respond to all the emails I receive.

Thank you
Sachin Sachdeva
Author and Illustrator

ISBN: 9798627517742

ISBN: 9781075214950

ISBN: 9781098834425

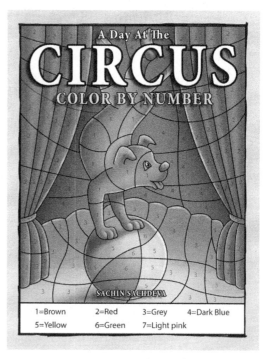

ISBN: 9781546514619

You might also like these Color By Number Books.
Search with their respective ISBN numbers.

ISBN: 9781075372476

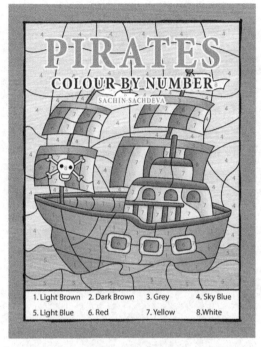

ISBN: 9781718941700

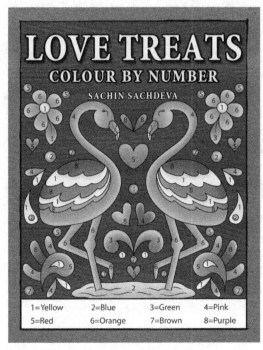

ISBN: 9781654940065

ISBN: 9781099409516

Join my Facebook Group for Freebies,
New Book launches and all the other updates.

Search for "Books by Sachin Sachdeva" on Facebook

I am also giving away Free 32 Coloring Pages PDF

 Type this link: https://tinyurl.com/yx4483nj

Made in the USA
Middletown, DE
23 October 2020